Guitar Chord Songbook

Nirvana

T0084125

Cover photo © Jeff Davey/Camera Press/Retna Ltd.

ISBN 978-1-4234-0691-4

HAL•LEONARD®
CORPORATION

7777 W. BLUEMOUND RD. P.O. BOX 13819 MILWAUKEE, WI 53213

Visit Hal Leonard Online at
www.halleonard.com

Guitar Chord Songbook

Contents

About a Girl

Words and Music by Kurt Cobain

Tune down 1/2 step:
(low to high) Eb–Ab–Db–Gb–Bb–Eb

Melody:

I need an eas-y friend, _

E5   G   C#   F#7add4   A   C

Intro   ‖: E5   G | E5   G   :‖ *Play 4 times*

Verse 1

E5 G   E5   G
I   need an easy friend,

E5 G   E5   G
I do, with an ear to lend.

E5 G   E5   G
I do   think you fit this shoe,

E5 G   E5   G
I do,   but you have a clue.

Chorus 1

C#   F#7add4
   I'll take ad-vantage while

C#   F#7add4
   You hang me out to dry,

   E5   A   C
But I can't see you ev'ry night

   E5 G   E5 G
For free.

   E5   G   E5   G
I do.

Verse 2

E5　G　　E5　　G
I'm standing in your line,

E5　G　　　E5　　　　G
I do, hope you have the time.

E5　G　　E5　　　G
I do, pick a number to,

E5　G　　E5　　　　G
I do, keep a date with you.

Chorus 2　　　*Repeat Chorus 1*

Guitar Solo　　*Repeat Verse 1 (Instrumental)*
　　　　　　　　Repeat Chorus 1 (Instrumental)

Verse 3　　　*Repeat Verse 1*

Chorus 3

C♯　　　　F♯7add4
　I'll take ad-vantage while

C♯　　　　　F♯7add4
　You hang me out to dry,

　E5　　　　　　A　C
But I can't see you ev'ry night.

E5　　　　　A　C
I can't see you ev'ry night

　E5　　G　E5　G
For free.

E5　　G　E5　G
I do.

E5　　G　E5　G
I do.

E5　　G　E5　G
I do.

E5
I do.

All Apologies

Words and Music by
Kurt Cobain

Melody:

What else   should I   be? ____

Drop D tuning, down 1/2 step:
(low to high) Db–Ab–Db–Gb–Bb–Eb

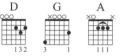

D   G   A

|**Intro**|‖: N.C.(D) | | | :‖|

Verse 1

N.C. (D)
What else should I be? All apologies.

What else should I say? Ev'ryone is gay.

What else could I write? I don't have the right.

What else should I be? All apologies.

Chorus 1

G
In the sun, in the sun I feel as one.

In the sun, in the sun.

A
Married, buried.

Verse 2

N.C. (D)
I wish I was like you, easily amused.

Find my nest of salt, ev'rything is my fault.

I'll take all the blame, aqua seafoam shame.

Sunburn, freezer burn, choking on the ashes of her enemy.

Chorus 2

G
  In the sun, in the sun I feel as one.

In the sun, in the sun.

A
Married, married.

Married, buried, yeah, yeah, yeah, yeah.

Interlude

| N.C.(D) | | | | |

Outro

N.C. (D)
‖: All alone is all we all are.

All alone is all we all are. :‖ *Play 5 times*

All alone is all we all,

All alone is all we all are.

All alone is all we all are.

Aneurysm

Words and Music by Kurt Cobain,
Krist Novoselic and David Grohl

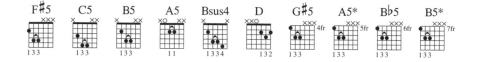

Come on o - ver and do the twist.

F#5 C5 B5 A5 Bsus4 D G#5 A5* Bb5 B5*

Intro

|F#5   C5 |B5   A5 |F#5 C5 |B5   A5 |

‖:N.C.(F#5) (C5) |(B5) (A5) |(F#5)(C5) |(B5)(A5) :‖

‖:F#5   C5 |B5   A5 |F#5 C5 |B5   A5 :‖ *Play 4 times*

‖:N.C.(F#5) | | | :‖

|B5 | | |Bsus4 |

|D | |B5 |Bsus4 |

|D | | |

Verse 1

B5   Bsus4   D
  Come on over and do the twist.   (Ah.) Ah, ha.

B5   Bsus4 D
  Overdo it and have a fit.   (Ah.)   Ah, ha.

B5   D
  Love you so much it makes me sick.   (Ah.)   Ah, ha.

B5   Bsus4   D
  Oh, come on over and do the twist.   (Ah.)   Ah, ha.

Chorus 1

F#5 G#5 A5* Bb5 B5*   Bb5 A5*
Beat me _____ out of me.

F#5 G#5 A5* Bb5 B5*   Bb5 A5*
‖: (Beat it, beat it.) Beat me _____ out of me. :‖ *Play 7 times*

Verse 2

B5   Bsus4   D
Come on over and do the twist.   (Ah.) Ah, ha.

B5   Bsus4   D
Overdo it and have a fit.   (Ah.) Ah, ha.

B5   Bsus4   D
Love you so much it makes me sick.   (Ah.) Ah, ha.

B5   Bsus4   D
Oh, come on over and shoot the shit.   (Ah.) Ah, ha.

Chorus 2   *Repeat Chorus 1*

Interlude |N.C.(F#5) | | | |
‖:N.C.(F#5) (C5) |(B5) (A5) |(F#5) (C5) |(B5) (A5) :‖
|F#5   C5 |B5   A5 |F#5   C5 |B5   A5 |

Bridge

F#5 C5   B5   A5
‖: She keeps it pump - in' straight _____ to my heart. :‖ *Play 8 times*

Outro   ‖:N.C.(F#5) | | | :‖   ‖

Been a Son

Words and Music by
Kurt Cobain

She should have   stayed _   a - way _ from   friends. _

Drop D tuning:
(low to high) D-A-D-G-B-E

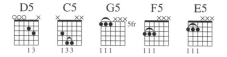

D5   C5   G5   F5   E5

Intro

| D5 N.C.(C5) D5 | N.C.(C5) | D5 N.C.(C5) D5 | N.C.(C5) |

Verse 1

D5 N.C.(C5)   D5   N.C.(C5)
She should have stayed away _____ from   friends.

D5 N.C.(C5)   D5   N.C.(C5)
She should have had more time _____ to spend.

D5 N.C.(C5)   D5   N.C.(C5)
She should have died when she _____ was born.

D5 N.C.(C5)   D5   N.C.(C5)   D5
She should have worn the crown _____ of thorns.

Chorus 1

N.C.(C5)   G5 F5   E5
She should have   been a son.

N.C.(C5)   G5 F5   E5
She should have   been a son.

N.C.(C5)   G5 F5   E5
She should have   been a son.

N.C.(C5)   G5 F5   E5   D5
She should have   been a son.

Verse 2

D5 N.C.(C5)   **D5**   **N.C.(C5)**
She should have stood out in ____ a crowd.

D5 N.C.(C5)   **D5**   **N.C.(C5)**
She should have made her moth - er   proud.

D5 N.C.(C5)   **D5**   **N.C.(C5)**
She should have fallen on ____ her stance.

D5 N.C.(C5)   **D5**   **N.C.(C5)**   **D5**
She should have had anoth - er chance.

Chorus 2   *Repeat Chorus 1*

Interlude | **D5 N.C.(C5) D5** | **N.C.(C5)** | **D5 N.C.(C5) D5** | **N.C.(C5)** |
                | **D5 N.C.(C5) D5** | **N.C.(C5)** | **D5 N.C.(C5) D5** |

Chorus 3   *Repeat Chorus 1*

Verse 3   *Repeat Verse 1*

Chorus 4

N.C.(C5)   **G5 F5**   **E5**
She should have   been a son.

N.C.(C5)   **G5 F5**   **E5**
She should have   been a son.

N.C.(C5)   **G5 F5**   **E5**
She should have   been a son.

N.C.(C5)   **G5 F5**   **E5**
She should have   been a son.

Big Cheese

Words and Music by
Kurt Cobain and Krist Novoselic

Melody:

Big cheese, ____

C5   B5   G   F#5   G5   B5*   Cm   B5**

Intro

‖: C5 B5 | C5 B5 | C5 B5 | C5 B5 :‖

| C5 B5 G | C5 B5 G | C5 B5 G | C5 B5 G |

Verse 1

C5 B5   G   C5 B5   G
    Big cheese,   make me.

C5 B5   G   C5 B5   G
    Mine says,   "Go to the office."

C5 B5   G   C5 B5   G
    Big cheese,   make me.

C5 B5   G   C5   B5
    Mine says,   "What'd they say?"

Chorus 1

F#5   G5
    Black is black, trading back.

F#5   G5
    We were enemies.

F#5   G5
    Sure you are, what am I?

F#5   G5
    Your enemies.

Verse 2

C5 B5   G   C5 B5   G
    Big lies,   make mine.

C5 B5   G   C5 B5   G
    Mine says,   "Go to the office."

C5 B5   G   C5 B5   G
    Big cheese,   make me.

C5 B5   G   C5 B5
    Mine says,   "What'd they say?"

Chorus 2

F#5   G5
Black is black, trading back.

F#5   G5
We were enemies.

F#5   G5   F#5   G5
She eats glue. How 'bout you?

Guitar Solo 1

‖:B5* N.C.(Cm) | B5* N.C.(Cm)   :‖ *Play 6 times*

Verse 3

C5 B5   G   C5 B5   G
      Big cheese,   make me.

C5 B5   G C5 B5   G
      Mine says,   "Go to the office."

C5 B5   G   C5 B5   G
      Big cheese,   make me.

C5 B5   G   C5 B5
      Mine says,   "Why'd they lie?"

Chorus 3

Repeat Chorus 2

Guitar Solo 2

Repeat Guitar Solo 1

Chorus 4

F#5   G5
Black is black, trading back.

F#5   G5
We were enemies.

F#5   G5
Sure you are, but what am I?

F#5   G5
We were enemies.

F#5   G5
She eats glue, how 'bout you?

F#5   G5
We were enemies.

F#5   G5   F#5   G5
Sure you are, what am I?

Outro

‖:B5* N.C.(Cm) | B5* N.C.(Cm)   :‖ *Play 4 times*
| B5** | | | |
| | | | | | ‖

Blew

Words and Music by
Kurt Cobain

Tune down 2 steps:
(low to high) C-F-Bb -Eb-G-C

Melody:

If you would-n't mind, __ I would like it blew. __

E5   G5   A5   Bb5   A7   B5   Em

Intro

| N.C. | | | | |

‖: E5   G5 A5 Bb5   A5 | G5   A5   :‖

Verse 1

N.C.(E5)   A7 N.C.(E5)   A7
    If you wouldn't mind, I would like it blew.

N.C.(E5)   A7 N.C.(E5)   A7
    If you wouldn't mind, I would like to lose.

N.C.(E5)   A7 N.C.(E5)   A7
    If you wouldn't care, I would like to leave.

N.C.(E5)   A7 N.C.(E5)   A7
    If you wouldn't mind, I would like to breathe.

Chorus 1

G5 A5   G5   A5   G5 Bb5
Is   there anoth - er   rea - son for your stain?

G5   A5   G5   A5   G5 Bb5
Could you believe who we knew was stress or   strain?

G5   A5   G5   A5   G5 A5   B5
Here is anoth - er word that rhymes with __ shame.

Verse 2   *Repeat Verse 1*

Chorus 2   *Repeat Chorus 1*

Guitar Solo   ‖: N.C.(Em) | | | :‖ *Play 4 times*

Chorus 3   *Repeat Chorus 1*

Outro

N.C.(E5)   (Bb5)   (A5)
‖:   You could do anything.   :‖ *Play 7 times*

N.C.(E5)   (Bb5) (A5) (E5) N.C.   E5
You could do any   -   thing.

Lithium

Words and Music by
Kurt Cobain

Melody:

I'm so hap-py 'cause to - day

Tune down 1 step:
(low to high) D-G-C-F-A-D

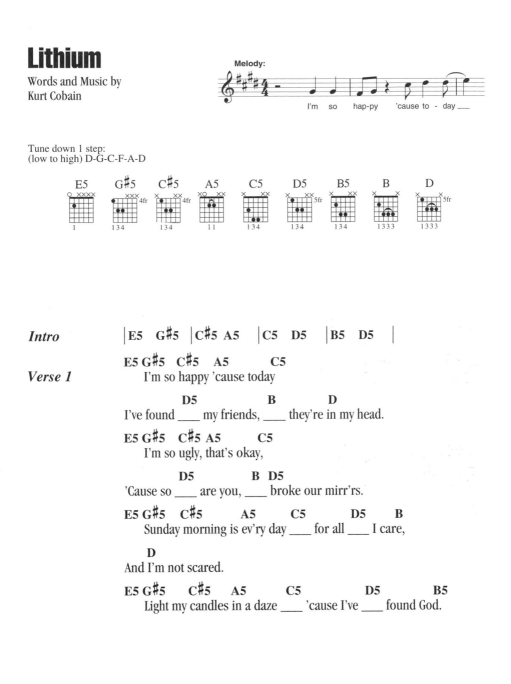

E5   G#5   C#5   A5   C5   D5   B5   B   D

Intro
|E5   G#5 |C#5   A5 |C5   D5 |B5   D5 |

Verse 1

E5 G#5   C#5   A5   C5
    I'm so happy 'cause today

          D5   B   D
I've found ___ my friends, ___ they're in my head.

E5 G#5   C#5 A5   C5
    I'm so ugly, that's okay,

          D5   B D5
'Cause so ___ are you, ___ broke our mirr'rs.

E5 G#5   C#5   A5   C5   D5   B
    Sunday morning is ev'ry day ___ for all ___ I care,

    D
And I'm not scared.

E5 G#5   C#5   A5   C5   D5   B5
    Light my candles in a daze ___ 'cause I've ___ found God.

Pre-Chorus 1

        D5 E5 G#5 C#5   A5   C5 D5 B5
Yeah, _____   yeah, ___ yeah.

        D5 E5 G#5 C#5   A5   C5 D5 B5
Yeah, _____   yeah, ___ yeah.

        D5 E5 G#5 C#5   A5   C5 D5 B5   D5
Yeah, _____   yeah, ___ yeah, _____ yeah.

Verse 2

E5 G#5 C#5 A5   C5
   I'm so lonely, that's okay,

        D5   B   D
I shaved ___ my head, ___ and I'm not sad.

E5 G#5   C#5 A5   C5
   And just maybe I'm to blame

        D5   B   D5
For all ___ I've heard, ___ but I'm not sure.

E5 G#5   C#5 A5   C5
   I'm so ex - cited, I can't wait

        D5   B   D
To meet ___ you there, ___ but I don't care.

E5 G#5 C#5 A5   C5   D5   B5
   I'm so horny, that's okay, ___ my will ___ is good.

Pre-Chorus 2   *Repeat Pre-Chorus 1*

Chorus 1

A5 C5   A5   C5
   I like it, I'm not gonna crack.

A5 C5   A5   C5
   I miss you, I'm not gonna crack.

A5 C5   A5   C5
   I love you, I'm not gonna crack.

A5 C5   A5   C5
   I'd kill you, I'm not gonna crack.

Chorus 2	A5 C5 A5 C5 I like it, I'm not gonna crack. A5 C5 A5 C5 I miss you, I'm not gonna crack. A5 C5 A5 C5 I love you, I'm not gonna crack. A5 C5 A5 C5 D5 B5 I'd kill you, I'm not gonna crack.
Interlude	|N.C.(E5) (G#5) |(C#5) (A5) |(C5) (D5) |(B5) (D5) |
Verse 3	*Repeat Verse 1*
Pre-Chorus 3	*Repeat Pre-Chorus 1*
Chorus 3	*Repeat Chorus 1*
Chorus 4	A5 C5 A5 C5 I like it, I'm not gonna crack. A5 C5 A5 C5 I miss you, I'm not gonna crack. A5 C5 A5 C5 I love you, I'm not gonna crack. A5 C5 A5 C5 D5 B5 E5 I'd kill you, I'm not gonna crack.

Breed

Words and Music by
Kurt Cobain

I don't care, I don't care, I don't care, I don't

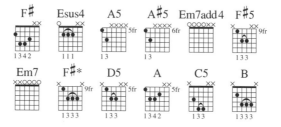

Intro

‖: F♯ Esus4 F♯ A5 A♯5 Em7add4 |

| F♯ Esus4 F♯ A5 A♯5 Em7add4 :‖ *Play 8 times*

Verse 1

F♯5
I don't care, I don't care, I don't care,

                                                    Em7
I don't care, I don't care, care if it's old.

F♯*
I don't mind, I don't mind, I don't mind,

                                       Em7
I don't mind, mind, don't have a mind.

F♯*
Get away, get away, get away,

                                   Em7
Get away, way, way from your home.

F♯*
I'm afraid, I'm afraid, I'm afraid,

                                F♯   Esus4 F♯   Em7add4
I'm afraid, 'fraid, (of a) ghost.

Chorus 1

D5   A   C5   B
Even if you have, even if you need…

D5   A   C5   B
I don't mean to stare. We don't have to breed.

D5   A   C5   B
We could plant a house. We could build a tree.

D5   A   C5   B
I don't e - ven care. We could have all three.

Bridge 1

               F# Esus4 F#   A5 A#5 Em7add4
She said, ‖: (She   said,) __   she said, :‖ *Play 6 times*

F# Esus4 F#5 A5 A#5 Em7add4 F# Esus4 F#5 A5 A#5 Em7add4
(She   said,) __   she said.

Verse 2   *Repeat Verse 1*

Chorus 2   *Repeat Chorus 1*

Bridge 2   *Repeat Bridge 1*

Guitar Solo ‖: F#   Esus4 F# A5 A#5 Em7add4 |
          | F#   Esus4 F# A5 A#5 Em7add4   :‖ *Play 8 times*

Chorus 3   *Repeat Chorus 1*

Bridge 3

               F# Esus4 F#   A5 A#5 Em7add4
She said, ‖: (She   said,) __   she said, :‖ *Play 7 times*

F# Esus4 F#5 A5 Em7add4 F#
(She   said,) __   she (Said.) said.

Come as You Are

Words and Music by
Kurt Cobain

Tune down 1 step:
(low to high) D-G-C-F-A-D

E5   F#m   Esus2   F#sus4   A   Bsus4   D5   D   F#sus4*

Intro

N.C.(E5) ‖: (F#m) |(E5)   :‖ *Play 4 times*

Verse 1

N.C.(F#m)   (E5)   (F#m)   (E5)
Come as you are, ___ as you were, ___ as I want ___ you to be;

(F#m)   (E5)   (F#m)   (E5)
   As a friend, ___ as a friend, ___ as an old ___ enemy.

(F#m)   (E5)   (F#m)   (E5)
   Take your time, ___ hurry up, ___ the choice is yours, ___ don't be late.

(F#m)   (E5)   (F#m)   (E5) Esus2
   Take a rest, ___ as a friend, ___ as an old ___ memory.

Bridge 1

F#sus4   A   F#sus4   A
   Ah, ___ memory, ___   ah, ___ memory,

F#sus4   A   F#sus4   A
   Ah, ___ memory, ___   ah.

Verse 2

N.C.(F#m)   (E5)   (F#m)   (E5)
Come doused in mud, ___ soaked in bleach, ___ as I want ___ you to be;

(F#m)   (E5)   (F#m)   (E5) Esus2
   As a trend, ___ as a friend, ___ as an old ___ memory.

Bridge 2   *Repeat Bridge 1*

Chorus 1

Bsus4 D5   Bsus4   D5
And I swear that I don't have a gun.

         Bsus4   D5   Bsus4   D5
No, I don't __ have a gun.   No, I don't __ have a gun.

Interlude   ‖: N.C.(F#m) |(E5)   :‖ *Play 2 times*

Guitar Solo   ‖: N.C.(F#m) |(E5)   :‖ *Play 7 times*
               |(F#m) |(E5) |

Bridge 3   *Repeat Bridge 1*

Chorus 2

Bsus4 D   Bsus4   D
And I swear that I don't have a gun.

         Bsus4   D   Bsus4   D
No, I don't __ have a gun. No, I don't __ have a gun.

         Bsus4   D5   Bsus4   D
No, I don't __ have a gun. No, I don't __ have a gun.

Outro

N.C.(F#m) (E5)   (F#m)   (E5)
               Memory, __   ah.

(F#m)   (E5)   (F#m)   (E5) F#sus4*
               Memory, __   ah.

Downer

Words and Music by
Kurt Cobain

Melody:

Spoken: Por - tray sin - cer - i - ty

Tune down 1/2 step:
(low to high) Eb - Ab - Db - Gb - Bb - Eb

E5   C5   C+   Bb5   B5   A5   E5*   F5

Intro
| N.C.(E5) (C5) | (E5)   (C5) | (E5)   (C5) | (E5)   C+ |
| E5   C5 | E5   C5 | E5   C5 | E5   C5 |

Verse 1

N.C.
Portray sincerity – act out of loyalty.

Defend your free country – wish away pain.

Hand out lobotomies to save little families.

            C+
Surrealistic fantasy bland, boring, plain.

Interlude 1
| E5   C5 | E5   C5 | E5   C5 | E5   C5 |

Chorus 1

Bb5 B5 C5 B5 Bb5 B5 C5 B5
Hold me now this res - ti - tu - tion,

Bb5 B5 C5 B5   Bb5 B5 C5 B5
Liv - ing out your date with fu - sion.

Bb5 B5 C5   B5   Bb5 B5 C5   B5
Is   the whole fleece shun in bas - tard?

Bb5 B5 C5   B5 Bb5 B5 C5   B5
Don't feel guilt - y   mas - ter writ - ing.

Interlude 2	*Repeat Interlude 1*

Bridge 1	A5 Bb5 E5* F5

A5   **Bb5**   **E5***   **F5**
Somebody said that they're not much __ like I am. I know I can.

A5   **Bb5**   **E5***   **F5**
Made e - nough up the words as __ you go along.__

I sing then some.

Interlude 3	*Repeat Interlude 1*

Verse 2	**N.C.** *Sickening pessimist hypocrite master.*

Conservative, communist, apocalyptic bastard.

Thank you, dear God, for putting me on this earth.

                                 C+
I feel very privileged in debt for my thirst.

Interlude 4	*Repeat Interlude 1*
Chorus 2	*Repeat Chorus 1*
Interlude 5	*Repeat Interlude 1*
Bridge 2	*Repeat Bridge 1*
Interlude 6	*Repeat Interlude 1*

Outro	|**N.C.(E5) (C5)** |**(E5) (C5)** |**(E5) (C5)** |**(E5) (C5)** |**(E5)** ||

Drain You

Words and Music by
Kurt Cobain

Melody:

One ba - by to ___ an-oth - er says _

Tune down 1step:
(low to high) D-G-C-F-A-D

B   D#   G#   C#   D#m   F#   E   A   G#sus4   G#5

1333   1333   1342   1333   1342   1342   231   111   1333   133

Verse 1

```
B      D#  G#   C#    B       D#m        G# C#
One ba - by to _ anoth - er says _ I'm luck - y to have met _ you.

B      D#m    G#      C#    B   D#m  G# C#
I don't _ care what _ you think _ unless _ it is _ about _ me.

B    D#m  G#   C#  B       D#m     G# C#
It is _ now _ my du - ty to _ complete - ly drain _ you.

B    D#m     G#      C#    B       D#m        G#   C#
A trav - el through _ a tube _ and end _ up in _ your infec - tion.
```

Chorus 1

```
F# E      C#        E       C#
   Chew your meat for you,   pass it back and forth.

E   C#      E       C#
In a passionate kiss,   from my mouth in yours.

B  A  G#sus4
I  like you.
```

Verse 2

```
B        D#m  G#  C#     B         D#m    G#  C#
With eyes _ so di - lat - ed I've _ become _ your pu - pil.

B          D#m  G#    C#     B    D#m  G#  C#
You've taught _ me ev - 'rything _ without _ a poi - son ap - ple.

B        D#m  G#    C#     B         D#m G#   C#
The wa - ter is _ so yel - low, I'm _ a health - y stu - dent.

B        D#m  G#    C#     B         D#m   G# C#
Indebt - ed and _ so grate - ful. Vac - uum out _ the flu - ids.
```

Chorus 2

```
F# E         C#       E     C#
    Chew your meat for you,   pass it back and forth.

E   C#        E          C#
In a passionate kiss,   from my mouth in yours.

B A  G#sus4
I  like you.
```

Interlude

```
‖: G#5    |         |           :‖  Play 6 times
| B  D#m  | G#  C# | B   D#m | G#  C#  |
```

Verse 3   *Repeat Verse 1*

Chorus 3

```
F# E         C#       E     C#
    Chew your meat for you,   pass it back and forth.

E   C#        E          C#
In a passionate kiss,   from my mouth in yours.

E     C#      E        C#
Sloppy lips to lips.   You're my vitamins.

B A  G#sus4
I  like you.
```

Dumb

Words and Music by Kurt Cobain

Tune down 1/2 step:
(low to high) Eb - Ab - Db - Gb - Bb - Eb

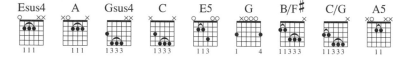

Verse 1

> Esus4 A　　　　　　Gsus4　C
> I'm not like them, __ I can pretend.

> Esus4 A　　　　　Gsus4　C
> The sun is gone, __ and I had a light.

> Esus4 A　　　　　Gsus4　C
> The day is done, __ but I'm havin' fun.

> Esus4 A　　　　　　Gsus4　C　　　　E5
> I think I'm dumb, __ 　maybe just happy.

Chorus 1

> E5 G　　　　　　E5
> Think I'm just happy.

> G　　　　E5
> Think I'm just happy.

> G　　　　　E5　　G
> Think I'm just happy.

Verse 2

> Esus4 A　　　　　　Gsus4　C
> My heart is broke, __ and I have some glue.

> Esus4 A　　　　　Gsus4　C
> Help me inhale, __ 　mend it with you.

> Esus4 A　　　　　　Gsus4　C
> We'll float around, __ 　hang out on clouds.

> Esus4 A　　　　　　Gsus4　C
> Then we'll come down, __ 　have a hangover.

Chorus 2

```
E5 G                      E5
    And have a hang - over.

G             E5
    Have a hang - over.

G             E5   G
    Have a hang - over.
```

Bridge

```
B/F♯          C/G        B/F♯          C/G
    Skin the sun, __ fall asleep.   Wish away, __ soul is cheap.

B/F♯              C/G          B/F♯              C/G
    Lesson learned, __ wish me luck.   Soothe the burn,   wake me up.
```

Verse 3

```
Esus4  A              Gsus4   C
    I'm not like them, __   and I can pretend.

Esus4  A              Gsus4   C
    The sun is gone, __  and I had a light.

Esus4  A              Gsus4   C
    The day is done, __ and I'm havin' fun.

Esus4  A              Gsus4   C
    I think I'm dumb, __    maybe just happy.
```

Chorus 3

```
E5 G                  E5
    I think I'm just happy.

G             E5
    I think I'm just happy.

G                 E5
    I think I'm just happy.
```

Outro

```
   E5  A5           G   C
‖: I think I'm dumb. __ I think I'm dumb. :‖ *Play 5 times*

E5  A5           G   C              E5
    I think I'm dumb. __ I think I'm dumb.
```

Floyd the Barber

Words and Music by Kurt Cobain

Melody:

Bell on a door clank, "Come on in."

Tune down 1/2 step:
(low to high) E♭ - A♭ - D♭ - G♭ - B♭ - E♭

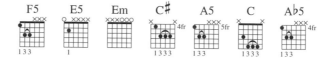

F5   E5   Em   C♯   A5   C   A♭5

Intro

‖: F5 E5 | F5 E5 | F5 E5 | F5 Em :‖

Verse 1

F5   E5   F5   E5
Bell on a door clank, "Come on in."

F5   E5   F5   Em
Floyd ob - serves my hairy chin.

F5   E5   F5   E5
"Sit down chair, don't be afraid."

F5   E5   F5   Em
Steamed, hot towel on my face.

Chorus 1

C♯ A5 C A♭5   C♯ A5 C A♭5
              I was shaved.

C♯ A5 C A♭5   C♯ A5 C5 A♭5
I was shamed._____ I was shamed.

Interlude 1

| F5 E5 | F5 E5 | F5 E5 | F5 Em |

Verse 2

```
F5     E5     F5            E5
```
Barney ties me to the chair.

```
F5     E5     F5            Em
```
I can't see, I'm really scared.

```
F5            E5     F5     E5
```
Floyd breathes hard I hear a zip.

```
F5     E5            F5     Em
```
Pee - pee pressed a - gainst my lips.

Chorus 2   *Repeat Chorus 1*

Guitar Solo   ‖: F5   │ N.C.(C) │ F5   │ N.C.(C) :‖

Interlude 2   *Repeat Interlude 1*

Verse 3

```
F5     E5     F5            E5
```
I sense others in the room.

```
F5 E5         F5     Em
```
Opie, Aunt Bea, I presume.

```
F5     E5            F5     E5
```
They take turns and cut me up.

```
F5 E5                F5     Em
```
I died smothered in Andy's butt.

Chorus 3

```
C♯  A5  C  A♭5        C♯  A5  C  A♭5
```
I was shaved.

```
    C♯  A5  C  A♭5      C♯  A5  C5  A♭5  F5  E5
```
I was shamed._____ I was shamed.

Frances Farmer Will Have Her Revenge on Seattle

Words and Music by
Kurt Cobain

Tune down 1/2 step:
(low to high) Eb - Ab - Db - Gb - Bb - Eb

Melody:

It's so re-liev - ing to know that you're leav - ing

(chord diagrams: G#5, E5, G5, B5, F#5, C5/G, C#5/G#, E5/B, D5/A)

(chord diagrams: B5/F#, Bb5/F, A, Bb5, G, E5*, C#5, C#/D)

Intro

| G#5 | E5 G5 | E5 G5 | G#5 | |
| E5 G5 | E5 G5 | B5 | F#5 G5 |

Verse 1

G#5   E5   G5   E5
It's so reliev - ing to know that you're leav - ing

G5   B5   F#5 G5
Soon as you __ get paid.

G#5   E5   G5   E5
It's so relax - ing to hear that you're ask - ing

G5   B5   E5 F#5
Wher - ever you get __ your way.

G5 G#5   E5   G5   E5
It's so sooth - ing to know that you'll sue __ me,

G5   B5   C5/G
Starting to sound __ the same.

Chorus 1

C#5/G#   E5/B   D5/A B5/F# C5/G
‖: I miss the comfort in being sad.   :‖

C#5/G#   E5/B   D5/A B5/F# Bb5/F A Bb5/F
I miss the comfort in being sad.

| B5   Bb5 | A | G | F#5   G5 |

Verse 2

G#5   E5   G5   E5
In her false wit - ness, we hope you're still with __ us

G5   B5   F#5 G5
To see if they float __ or drown.

G#5   E5   G5   E5
Our favorite pa - tient, display of pa - tience,

G5   B5   F#5 G5
Dis - ease covered Pu - get Sound.

G#5   E5   G5   E5
She'll come back as fire __ to burn all the li - ars,

G5   B5   C5
Leave a blanket of ash __ on the ground.

Chorus 2   *Repeat Chorus 1*

Interlude   ‖: G#5 E* |G#5 E* |G#5 E* |C#5 |C#/D :‖ *Play 3 times*
|B5 Bb5|A |G |F#5 G5|

Verse 3

G#5   E5   G5   E5
It's so reliev - ing to know that you're leav - ing

G5   B5   F# G5
Soon as you __ get paid.

G#5   E5   G5   E5
It's so relax - ing to know that you're ask - ing

G5   B5   F#5 G5
Wher - ever you get __ your way.

G#5   E5   G5   E5
It's so sooth - ing to know that you'll sue __ me,

G5   B5   C5
Starting to sound __ the same.

Chorus 3

C#5/G#   E5/B   D5/A B5/F# C5/G
‖: I miss the comfort in being sad.   :‖

C#5/G#   E5/B   D5/A B5/F#   Bb5/F A Bb/F
I miss the comfort in being sad.

|B5 Bb|A |G |F#5 G5|G#5 | ‖

Heart Shaped Box

Words and Music by
Kurt Cobain

Melody:

She _ eyes me   like ___   a   Pis - ces   when _

Drop D tuning, down 1/2 step:
(low to high) Db - Ab - Db - Gb - Bb - Eb

A5   F5   D5   D7   A

| 1 1 | 1 1 1 | | 2 3 | 1 1 1 |

Intro |A5 F5 |D5 |A5 F5 |D7 |

Verse 1
```
A      F5          D5                   A5  F5          D7
She eyes me like ___ a Pisces when ___ I ___ am weak.

A          F5          D5                        A    F5      D7
I've been locked inside ___ your heart shaped box ___ for ___ weeks.

A          F5          D5                   A    F5      D7
I've been drawn into ___ your magnet tar ___ pit ___ trap.

A          F5          D5                   A5  F5              D7
I wish I could eat ___ your cancer when ___ you ___ turn black.
```

Chorus 1
```
        A5    F5      D7
||:    Hey!  Wait!    I've got a new complaint.

A5      F5          D7
For - ever in debt ___ to your priceless advice. :||

A5      F5    D7
Hey!   Wait!    I've got a new complaint.

A5      F5          D7                            F5  D5          F5  D7
For - ever in debt ___ to your priceless advice, ___      your advice.
```

Verse 2

     A   **F5**   **D5**   **A**   **F5**   **D7**
Meat - eating or - chids forgive no __ one __ just yet.

     A   **F5**   **D5**   **A**   **F5**   **D7**
Cut my - self on an - gel's hair and ba - by's __ breath.

     A   **F5**   **D5**   **A**   **F5**   **D7**
Broken hymen of __ your highness, I'm __ left __ black.

     A   **F5**   **D5**   **A**   **F5**   **D7**
Throw down your umbil - ical noose so I can   climb __ right back.

Chorus 2   *Repeat Chorus 1*

Guitar Solo ‖: A5 F5 |D5 |A5 F5 |D5   :‖

Verse 3   *Repeat Verse 1*

      A5 **F5**   **D7**
Chorus 3 ‖: Hey! Wait!   I've got a new complaint.

     A5 **F5**   **D7**
For - ever in debt __ to your priceless advice. :‖

     A5 **F5**   **D7**
Hey! Wait!   I've got a new complaint.

     A5 **F5**   **D7**
For - ever in debt __ to your priceless advice,

     F5 **D5**   **F5** **D5**   **F5** **D5**   **F5** **D7**
Your advice, __   your advice, __   your advice.

In Bloom

Words and Music by
Kurt Cobain

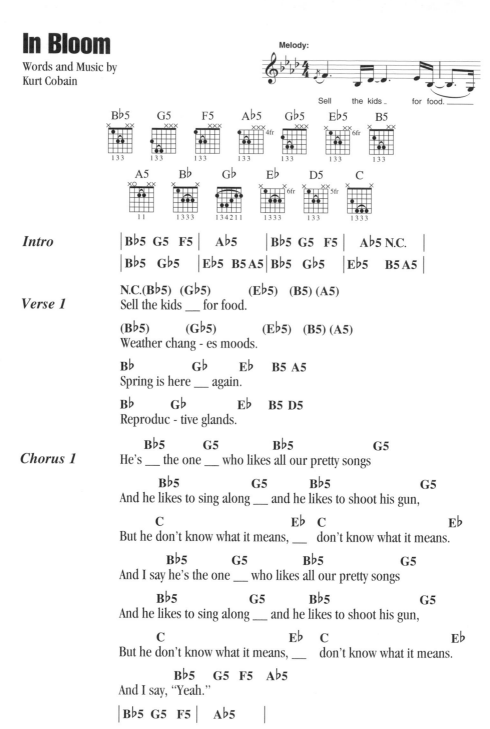

Intro

|Bb5 G5 F5 | Ab5 |Bb5 G5 F5 | Ab5 N.C. |
|Bb5 Gb5 |Eb5 B5 A5|Bb5 Gb5 |Eb5 B5 A5 |

Verse 1

N.C.(Bb5) (Gb5)   (Eb5) (B5) (A5)
Sell the kids __ for food.

(Bb5)   (Gb5)   (Eb5) (B5) (A5)
Weather chang - es moods.

Bb   Gb   Eb   B5 A5
Spring is here __ again.

Bb   Gb   Eb   B5 D5
Reproduc - tive glands.

Chorus 1

        Bb5   G5   Bb5   G5
He's __ the one __ who likes all our pretty songs

        Bb5   G5   Bb5   G5
And he likes to sing along __ and he likes to shoot his gun,

        C   Eb C   Eb
But he don't know what it means, __ don't know what it means.

        Bb5   G5   Bb5   G5
And I say he's the one __ who likes all our pretty songs

        Bb5   G5   Bb5   G5
And he likes to sing along __ and he likes to shoot his gun,

        C   Eb C   Eb
But he don't know what it means, __ don't know what it means.

        Bb5   G5 F5 Ab5
And I say, "Yeah."

|Bb5 G5 F5 | Ab5 |

Verse 2

N.C.(B♭5) (G♭5)   (E♭5) (B5) (A5)
We can have __ some more.

(B♭5) (G♭5)   (E♭5) (B5) (A5)
Nature is __ a whore.

B♭   G♭   E♭ B5 A5
Bruises on __ the fruit.

B♭   G♭   E♭ B5 D5
Tender age __ in bloom.

Chorus 2   *Repeat Chorus 1*

Guitar Solo   ‖: N.C.(B♭5) (G♭5) |(E♭5) (B5) (A5) :‖ *Play 3 times*
|(B♭5)   (G♭5) |(E♭5) B5 E♭5 D5 |

Chorus 3

   B♭5   G♭5   B♭5   G5
He's __ the one __ who likes all our pretty songs

    B♭5   G5   B♭5   G5
And he likes to sing along __ and he likes to shoot his gun,

    C   E♭ C   E♭
But he don't know what it means, __ don't know what it means.

    B♭5   G5   B♭5   G5
And I say he's the one __ who likes all our pretty songs

    B♭5   G5   B♭5   G5
And he likes to sing along __ and he likes to shoot his gun,

    C   E♭ C   E♭
But he don't know what it means, __ don't know what it means,

C   E♭ C   E♭
Don't know what it means, __ don't know what it means.

    B♭5 G5 F5 A♭5 B♭5 G5 F5 A♭5 B♭5
And I say, "Yeah."

Jesus Doesn't Want Me for a Sunbeam

Words and Music by
Frances McKee and Eugene Kelly

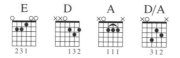

Melody:

Je - sus ____ don't want me for ____ a sun - beam. ____

Tune down 1/2 step:
(low to high) E♭ - A♭ - D♭ - G♭ - B♭ - E♭

E   D   A   D/A

2 3 1   1 3 2   1 1 1   3 1 2

Intro

‖: E |D |A   D/A |A   :‖

Verse 1

E   D   A   D/A A
Jesus don't want me for a sun - beam.

E   D   A   D/A A
Sunbeams are never made like me.

E   D   A   D/A   A
Don't expect me to cry __ for all the reasons you have to die.

E   D   A   D/A A
Don't ever ask your love of me.

Chorus 1

E   D   E   D
Don't expect me to cry. Don't expect me to lie.

E   D   A   D/A A
Don't expect me to die for me.

Verse 2	*Repeat Verse 1*
Chorus 2	*Repeat Chorus 1*

Interlude   ‖: E |D |A   D/A|A   :‖

Chorus 3	*Repeat Chorus 1*
Verse 3	*Repeat Verse 1*

Chorus 4

E   D E   D
Don't expect me to cry. Don't expect me to lie.

E   D E   D
Don't expect me to die. Don't expect me to cry.

E   D E   D   A D/A A
Don't expect me to lie. Don't expect me to die for me.

Outro   ‖: E |D |A   D/A|A   :‖

Lounge Act

Words and Music by
Kurt Cobain

Melody:

Truth   cov-ered in se - cu - ri - ty, ____

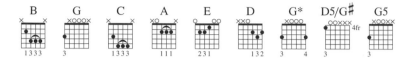

B   G   C   A   E   D   G*   D5/G#   G5

Intro

|N.C.(B) (G)| (C) |(B)   (G)| (C) |
|B   G | C |B   G | C |

Verse 1

      B   G   C
Truth   covered in security,

B G   C
    I can't let you smother me.

B G   C
    I'd like to but it couldn't work,

B G   C
    Trading off and taking turns.

B G   C   A
    I don't regret a thing.

Chorus 1

                    E   A   D   G*
And I've got __ this friend, you see, __ who makes me feel,

E   A   D   G*
    And I wanted more ____ than I could steal.

E   A   D   G*
    I'll ar - rest myself, ____ I'll wear a shield.

E   A   D   G*
    I'll go out of my way ____ to prove

  A   D5/G# G5   A   D5/G# G5
I still   smell her on you.

Verse 2

    B   **G**   **C**
Don't   tell me what I want to hear.

    B G   **C**
    Afraid of nev - er knowing fear,

    B G   **C**
    Experience an - ything you need.

    B G   **C**
    I'll keep fight - ing jealousy

    B G   **C**
    Until it's fucking gone.

Chorus 2   *Repeat Chorus 1*

Interlude | **B**   **G** | **C** | **B**   **G** | **C** |

Verse 3   *Repeat Verse 1*

             E   **A**   **D**   **G**
Chorus 3   And I've got __ this friend, you see, __ who makes me feel

    E   **A**   **D**   **G**
    And I wanted more __ than I could steal.

    E   **A**   **D**   **G**
    I'll ar - rest myself, ____ I'll wear a shield.

    E   **A**   **D**   **G**
    I'll go out of my way ____ to make you a deal.

    E   **A**   **D**   **G**
    We'll make a pact ____ to learn from

       E   **A**   **D**   **G**
Who - ever, ever we want __ with - out new rules

    E   **A**   **D**   **G**
    And we'll share what's lost __ and what we grew.

    E   **A**   **D** **G**
Outro   They'll go out of their way __ to prove

      A **D5/G♯** **G5**   **A**   **D5/G♯** **G5**
They still   smell her on ____ you.

      A **D5/G♯** **G5**   **A**   **D5/G♯** **G5**
They still   smell her on ____ you,

        A
Smell her on __ you.

The Man Who Sold the World

Words and Music by David Bowie

Melody:

We passed up - on the stairs, ___

Tune down 1/2 step:
(low to high) Eb–Ab–Db–Gb–Bb–Eb

F Dm A C Db

134211 231 123 32 1 1333

Intro

| N.C. | | | | | |
| F | | | Dm | | |

Verse 1

            A
We passed upon the stairs,

            Dm
We spoke in walls and web.

            A
Although I wasn't there,

            F
He said I was his friend,

            C
Which came as a surprise.

            A
I spoke into his eyes.

            Dm
I thought you died a long,

            C
A long, long time ago.

Chorus 1	C F Oh no, __ not me,

      C   F
Chorus 1   Oh no, __ not me,

      D♭   F
    We never lost control.

         C   F
    The face ____ to face

      D♭
    Of a man who sold the world.

Interlude 1

A		Dm		
F		Dm	N.C.	

                    A
Verse 2   I laughed and shook his hand

                         Dm
    And made my way back home.

               A
    I searched afar the land,

                     F
    For years and years I roamed.

            C
    I gazed a gazy stare.

            A
    We walked a million hills.

            Dm
    I must have died a long,

            C
    A long, long time ago.

Chorus 2

        C   **F**
Who knows? Not me.

      D♭   **F**
I never lost control.

         C   **F**
You're face ____ to face

         D♭
With the man who sold the world.

| **A** | | **Dm** | |

Chorus 3

        C   **F**
Who knows? ____ Not me.

      D♭   **F**
We never lost control.

         C   **F**
You're face ____ to face

         D♭
With the man who sold the world.

Interlude 2

| **A** | | **Dm** | |
| **F** | | |

Guitar Solo

Dm		**A**	
Dm		**F**	
Dm		**A**	
Dm		**F**	
Dm		**A**	
Dm		**F**

On a Plain

Words and Music by
Kurt Cobain

Melody:

I'll start this _ off _ with-out an - y words. _

Drop D tuning:
(low to high) D-A-D-G-B-E

B(♭5)/D♯   D   G5   F5   E5   F5*   C5

B5   A5   B♭maj7sus2   F5**   E5*   D5   G5*

Intro
```
|B(♭5)/D♯   |           |          | N.C.     |
```

Verse 1

```
D   G5          F5      E5 F5* E5
```
I'll start this off ____with - out an - y words.

```
D  G5          F5         E5      F5* E5
```
I got so high ____ (that) I scratched till I bled.

```
D  C5         B5  A5
```
I love myself ____ better than you.

```
D   G5             F5      E5 F5*   E5
```
I know it's wrong. ____ So, what should I do?

Verse 2

```
D    G5         F5      E5 F5* E5
```
The finest day ____ that I've ev - er had

```
D    G5            F5      E5 F5* E5
```
Was when I learned ____ to cry on command.

```
D  C5         B5  A5
```
I love myself ____ better than you.

```
D  G5             F5      E5  F5*    E5
```
I know it's wrong. ____ So, what should I do?

Chorus 1

D G5 Bbmaj7sus2
(Oo.) ___ I'm on a plain.

D G5 Bbmaj7sus2
(Oo.) ___ I can't complain.

D G5 Bbmaj7sus2
(Oo.) ___ I'm on a plain.

D G5 Bbmaj7sus2
(Oo.)

Verse 3

D   G5   F5 E5 F5* E5
My mother died ___ ev - er - y night.

D   G5   F5   E5   F5* E5
It's safe to say, ___ (don't) quote me   on that.

D   C5   B5 A5
I love myself ___ better than you.

D G5   F5   E5 F5*   E5
I know it's wrong. ___ So, what should I do?

Verse 4

D   G5   F5 E5   F5*   E5
The black sheep got ___ black - mailed again.

D   G5   F5 E5 F5* E5
For - got to put ___ on the   zip code.

D   C5   B5 A5
I love myself ___ better than you.

D G5   F5   E5 F5*   E5
I know it's wrong. ___ So, what should I do?

Chorus 2   *Repeat Chorus 1*

Bridge

F5**   E5*   D5 A5 G5* D5
Somewhere I have heard this be - fore

F5** E5*   D5 A5   G5* D5
In a dream my mem'ry has ___ stored.

F5**   E5*   D5 A5   G5* D5
As de - fense I neutered and ___ spayed.

F5**   E5*   D5 A5 G5 N.C.
What the hell am I trying to   say?

Verse 5

```
D   G5          F5    E5   F5*  E5
```
It is now time ___ to make it   unclear,

```
D   G5          F5    E5   F5*  E5
```
To write off lines ___ that don't make ___ sense.

```
D   C5         B5  A5
```
I love myself ___ better than you.

```
D   G5              F5    E5  F5*   E5
```
I know it's wrong. ___ So, what should I do?

Verse 6

```
D G5            F5 E5   F5*  E5
```
One more spe - cial mes - sage to go

```
D    G5            F5       E5 F5*  E5
```
And then I'm done, ___ then I   can go home.

```
D   C5         B5  A5
```
I love myself ___ better than you.

```
D   G5              F5    E5  F5*    E5
```
I know it's wrong. ___ So, what should I do?

Chorus 3

```
D   G5   Bbmaj7sus2
```
(Oo.) ___ I'm on a plain.

```
D   G5   Bbmaj7sus2
```
(Oo.) ___ I can't complain.

```
 D G5   Bbmaj7sus2
```
‖: (Oo.) ___ I'm on a plain.

```
D   G5   Bbmaj7sus2
```
(Oo.) ___ I can't complain. :‖ *Repeat and fade*

Mexican Seafood

Words and Music by
Kurt Cobain

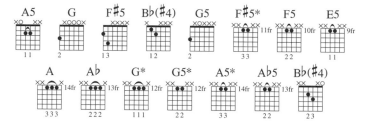

Melody:

Uh, the itch-y flakes, it is a flam-ing.

Tune down 1/2 step:
(low to high) Eb-Ab-Db-Gb-Bb-Eb

| A5 | G | F#5 | Bb(#4) | G5 | F#5* | F5 | E5 |

| A | Ab | G* | G5* | A5* | Ab5 | Bb(#4) |

Intro

‖: **A5   G   F#5** ｜   :‖ *Play 4 times*

Verse 1

Bb(#4) N.C.   Bb(#4) N.C.   Bb(#4) G5
Uh,   the itchy flakes,   it is a flam   -   ing.

Bb(#4) N.C.   Bb(#4) N.C.   Bb(#4) G5
To   the gels and creams,   it is per - tain   -   ing

Bb(#4) N.C.   Bb(#4) N.C.   Bb(#4) G5
To   a fungus mold   cured by in - jec   -   tion.

Bb(#4) N.C.   Bb(#4) N.C.   Bb(#4) G5
Hope   it's only a,   a yeast in - fec   -   tion.

Chorus 1

A5 G F#5   A5   G F#5
          Only hurts ___ when I,

          A5 G F#5
Hurts when I pee.

                    A5   G5 F#5
Only hurts ___ when I,

                    A5 G F#5
Hurts when I see.

Verse 2

Bb(#4) N.C.   Bb(#4) N.C.   Bb(#4) G5
Now   I vomit cum   and diar - rhe - a

Bb(#4) N.C.   Bb(#4) N.C.   Bb(#4) G5
On   the tile floor   like oatmeal piz   - za.

Bb(#4) N.C.   Bb(#4) N.C.   Bb(#4) G5 Bb(#4) N.C.
Fill   my toilet bowl   full of a cloud - y   puss,

            Bb(#4) N.C.   Bb(#4) G5
I feel the blood   becoming chow - der rust.

Chorus 2   *Repeat Chorus 1*

|A5 F#5* F5 E5 A Ab G* F#5* G5* |
||:A5 F#5* F5 E5 A5* Ab5 G5*   F#5* G5* :||
|A5 F#5* F5 E5 A Ab5 G5* |
||:N.C. | :||

Bb(#4) N.C.   Bb(#4) N.C.   Bb(#4) G5
Roll   into my bed,   which does consist of

Verse 3

Bb(#4) N.C.   Bb(#4) N.C.   Bb(#4) G5
Lice,   bugs and fleas   and yellow mu   - cus.

Bb(#4) N.C.   Bb(#4) N.C.   Bb(#4) G5
Stained   dirt, vase - line,   toe jam and boo - ger

Bb(#4) N.C.   Bb(#4) N.C.   Bb(#4) G5
Stom   - ach acid worms   that dance in sug - ared sludge.

Bb(#4) N.C. G5 Bb(#4) N.C. G5
Ah.

Outro

Bb(#4) N.C. G5 Bb(#4) N.C. G5 Bb(#4)*
Ah._____   Ah.

Milk It

Words and Music by
Kurt Cobain

Tune down 1/2 step:
(low to high) Eb - Ab - Db - Gb - Bb - Eb

Melody:

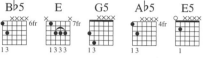

I am ___ my own par-a-site.   I don't need _ a

Bb5   E   G5   Ab5   E5

Intro

‖: N.C. (Bb5) (E) (G5) (Ab5) (E5) | (Bb5) (E5) (G5)   :‖

‖: Bb5   E   G5   Ab5   E5 | Bb5   E   G5   N.C.   :‖

| Bb5   E   G5   Ab5   E5 | Bb5   E   G5   Ab5   E5 |

‖: N.C. (Bb5) (E) (G5) (Ab5) (E5) | (Bb5) (E) (G5) (Ab5) (E5) :‖

Verse 1

N.C. (Bb5) (E)   (G5)   (Ab5)   (E5)
     I _____ am ___ my own ___ par - asite.

(Bb5) (E)   (G5)   (Ab5) (E5)
    I   don't need ___ a host to ___   live.

(Bb5) (E)   (G5)   (Ab5)   (E5)
    We ___ feed ___ off of each ___ oth - er.

(Bb5) (E)   (G5)   (E5)
    We   can share ___ our endorphins.

Pre-Chorus 1

| Bb5   E   G5   Ab5   E5 | Bb5   E   G5   N.C.

    Bb5   E   G5   Ab5   E5   Bb5   E   G5   N.C.
Doll steak,

    Bb5   E   G5   Ab5   E5   Bb5   E   G5   Ab5   E5
Test meat!

Chorus 1

Bb5   E   G5   E5
Look ___ on the bright side (is) suicide.

Bb5   E   G5   E5
Lost ___ eyesight, I'm on your side.

Bb5   E   G5   E5
An - gel left wing, right wing, broken wing.

Bb5   E   G5   E5
Lack of iron and or sleeping.

Interlude 1 ‖: N.C. (B♭5) (E) (G5) (A♭5) (E5) :‖

Verse 2

N.C. (B♭5) (E)   (G5)   (A♭5) (E5)
   I _____ own ___ my own pet ___ vi - rus.
(B♭5) (E)   (G5)   (A♭5)   (E5)
   I _____ get ___ to pet and ___ name ___ her.
(B♭5) (E)   (G5)   (A♭5) (E5)
   Her ___ milk ___ is my ___ shit.
(B♭5) (E)   (G5)   (E5)
   My ___ shit ___ is ___ her milk.

Pre-Chorus 2

|B♭5 E G5 A♭5 E5 | B♭5 E G5 N.C.

  B♭5 E G5 A♭5 E5 B♭5 E G5 N.C.
Test meat,
    B♭5 E G5 A♭5 E5 B♭5 E G5 A♭5 E5
Doll steak!

Chorus 2 *Repeat Chorus 1*

Interlude 2 ‖: N.C. (B♭5) (E) (G5) (A♭5) (E5) :‖ *Repeat 8 times*

Pre-Chorus 3

|B♭5 E G5 A♭5 E5 | B♭5 E G5 N.C.

  B♭5 E G5 A♭5 E5 B♭5 E G5 N.C.
Doll steak,
    B♭5 E G5 A♭5 E5 B♭5 E G5 A♭5 E5
Mm, test meat!

Chorus 3

B♭5   E   G5   E5
  Look ___ on the bright side (is) suicide.
B♭5   E   G5   E5
  Lost ___ eyesight, I'm on your side.
B♭5   E   G5   E5
  An - gel left wing, right wing, broken wing.
B♭5   E   G5   E5
  Lack of iron and or sleeping.
B♭5   E   G5   E5
  Pro - tector of the kennel.
B♭5   E   G5   E5
  Ec - toplasma, ecto - skeletal,
B♭5   E   G5 E5
  O - bitu - ary birthday.
   B♭5   E   G5   E5   G5
Your scent is still ___ here (in) my place of re - covery.

Mr. Moustache

Words and Music by
Kurt Cobain

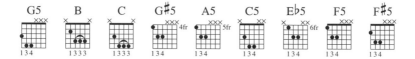

Intro

‖: N.C. | :‖ *Play 4 times*

‖: G5   N.C. | G5   N.C. :‖

Verse 1

G5   N.C. G5   N.C.
Fill me in on your new vision,

G5   N.C.   G5   N.C.
Wake me up with inde - cision.

G5   N.C.   G5   N.C.
Help me trust your mighty wisdom,

G5   N.C.   G5   N.C.
Yes, I eat cow, I am not proud.

Interlude 1

‖: N.C. | :‖

Verse 2

G5   N.C.   G5   N.C.
Show me how you question question,

G5   N.C.   G5   N.C.
Lead the way to my temp - tation.

G5   N.C.   G5   N.C.
Take my hand and give it cleaning,

G5   N.C.   G5   N.C.
Yes, I eat cow, I am not proud.

Interlude 2

‖: N.C. | :‖ *Play 4 times*

Bridge 1	**B C G5** Easy in an easy chair.
	B C G5 **N.C.** Poop as hard as rock.
	B C G5 I don't like you anyway.
	B C G5 **G♯5** Seal it in a box.

Chorus 1

|**A5**   **G5**|**A5**   **G5**|

C5 E♭5
Now you.

|**A5** **G♯5 G5**|**A5** **G♯5 G5**|

C5 E♭5
Now you.

Intterlude 3

‖: **N.C.** | :‖
‖: **G5** **N.C.** | **G5** **N.C.** :‖

Verse 3	*Repeat Verse 1*
Interlude 4	*Repeat Interlude 1*
Verse 4	*Repeat Verse 2*
Interlude 5	*Repeat Interlude 2*
Bridge 2	*Repeat Bridge 1*
Chorus 2	*Repeat Chorus 1*

Chorus 3

|**A5** **G♯5 G5**|**A5** **G♯5 G5**|

C5 E♭5
Now you.

|**A5** **G♯5 G5**|**A5** **G♯5 G5**|

C5 E♭5
Now you.

Outro

‖: **N.C.** | | | :‖ *Play 3 times*
 | | | **F5 F♯5**|

G5   ‖

Negative Creep

Words and Music by
Kurt Cobain

Melody:

This is out of our reach, this is out of our reach,

Tune down 1 step:
(low to high) D-G-C-F-A-D

E   E5   G#5   Bm   Bb5

Intro

‖: N.C.(E) | | | :‖

Verse 1

N.C.(E)
This is out of our reach, this is out of our reach,

This is out of our reach. Grown.

This is getting to be, this is getting to be, this is getting to be drone.

I'm a negative creep, I'm a negative creep,

I'm a negative creep and I'm stoned.

I'm a negative creep, I'm a negative creep,

I'm a negative creep and I am…

Chorus 1

| E5 G#5 | B5 Bb5 |
| E5 G#5 | B5 Bb5 |
Oh.

   E5   G#5   B5   Bb5
‖: Daddy's lit - tle girl ain't a girl no _____ more. :‖ *Play 6 times*

Verse 2	**N.C.(E)** This is out of our reach, this is out of our reach,
	This is out of our reach. And it's crude.
	This is getting to be, this is getting to be, this is getting to be a drone.
	I'm a negative creep, I'm a negative creep,
	I'm a negative creep and I'm stoned.
	I'm a negative creep, I'm a negative creep,
	I'm a negative creep and I am…
Chorus 2	*Repeat Chorus 1*

Interlude

N.C.(E)				
			Yeah!	

N.C.(E)				
			Drone!	

N.C.(E)				
			Stoned!	

N.C.(E)			**E5**	

Outro-Chorus

    E5   **G#5**
‖: Daddy's lit - tle girl

    B5   **Bb5**
Ain't a girl no _____ more. :‖ *Repeat and fade*

Pennyroyal Tea

Words and Music by
Kurt Cobain

Melody:

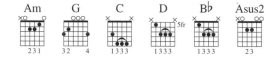

I'm on ____ my time ____ with

Tune down 1/2 step:
(low to high) E♭ - A♭ - D♭ - G♭ - B♭ - E♭

Am   G   C   D   B♭   Asus2

Verse 1

> **Am**   **G**
> I'm on my time with ev'ryone.
>
> **Am**   **G**
> I have very bad posture.

Chorus 1

> **C**   **D**   **B♭**
> Sit and drink   pennyroyal tea.
>
> **C**   **D**   **B♭**
> Distill the life that's inside of me.
>
> **C**   **D**   **B♭**
> Sit and drink   pennyroyal tea.
>
> **C**   **D**   **B♭**
> I'm ane - mic royal - ty.

Verse 2

> **Am**   **G**
> Give me a Leonard Cohen afterworld,
>
> **Am**   **G**
> So I can sigh e - ternally.

Chorus 2

```
C          D        Bb
I'm so tir - ed I can't sleep.

C          D        Bb
I'm a li - ar and a thief.

C               D            Bb
I sit and drink    pennyroyal tea.

C          D        Bb
I'm ane - mic royal - ty.
```

Interlude

‖: **Am** | | **G** | :‖

‖: **C** | **D** | **Bb** | :‖

Verse 3

```
Am                   G
I'm on warm milk and laxatives,

Am               G
Cherry flavored ant - acids.
```

Chorus 3   *Repeat Chorus 1*

Outro

```
Asus2 Am Asus2   Am Asus2 Am Asus2 Am
         I'm...     I'm...     I'm...

Asus2 Am Asus2   Am Asus2 Am Asus2
I'm...    I'm...    I'm...    I'm...
```

Plateau

Written by
Curt Kirkwood

Melody:

Man-y a hand _ has scaled the grand _ old

Tune down 1/2 step:
(low to high) Eb - Ab - Db - Gb - Bb - Eb

G   Bb   Fsus2   Abmaj7   G5   Bb*   Bb/F

Abmaj7add#4   Bb6   Aadd9   Dmaj7   C6/9   Fadd#4

Intro

‖: G   Bb   G   Bb | G   Bb   Fsus2 :‖ *Play 4 times*

Verse 1

G　　　　Bb　　G　　　　Bb
Many a hand ___ has scaled the grand

　　　G　　　Bb　　Fsus2
Old face of the ___ plateau.

G　　　　Bb　　G　　Bb
Some belong ___ to strangers,

　　　G　　　　Bb　　　Fsus2
And some to folks ___ you know.

G Bb　　　G　　　Bb
Holy ghosts and talk show hosts

　　　G　　　Bb　　Fsus2
Are planted in ___ the sand.

G　　　Bb　　G　　Bb
Beautify ___ the foothills,

G　　　Bb　　　Fsus2 Abmaj7
Shake the many hands.

Chorus 1

G5　　　　　　　　　　Bb*　　　Bb/F
Nothing on the top but a bucket and a mop

　　　G5　　　　　　　Bb*
And an illustrated book about birds.

　　　　G5　　　　　　Bb*　　Bb/F
You see a lot up there, but don't be scared.

G5　　　　　　Bb*
Who needs action when you got words?

Interlude 1   ‖: G B♭ G B♭ |G B♭ Fsus2   :‖

Verse 2
      G   B♭   G   B♭
When you've finished with the mop then you can stop

     G   B♭   Fsus2
And look at what ____ you've done.

      G   B♭   G   B♭
The plateau's clean, no dirt to be seen,

          G   B♭   Fsus2 A♭maj7
And the work, it was fun.

Chorus 2   *Repeat Chorus 1*

Interlude 2   *Repeat Interlude 1*

Verse 3
G   B♭   G   B♭
Many a hand ____ be - gan to scan

         G   B♭   Fsus2
Around ____ for the next pla - teau.

G   B♭   G   B♭
Some say ____ it was Greenland,

G   B♭   Fsus2
Some say Mexi - co.

G   B♭   G   B♭
Others decid - ed it ____ was nowhere,

       G   B♭   Fsus2
Ex - cept for where ____ they stood.

G   B♭   G   B♭
Those were all ____ just guesses,

        G   B♭   Fsus2
Wouldn't help you if they could.

|A♭maj7add♯4 |B♭6 |

Outro   ‖: Aadd9 |Dmaj7 C⁶ₙ |Aadd9 |Fadd♯4 C⁶ₙ :‖ *Play 4 times*
       Ooh,   ooh.   Ooh,   ooh.

|Asus2   ‖

(New Wave) Polly

Words and Music by
Kurt Cobain

Melody:

Pol - ly wants a crack - er,

Esus4   G   D   C   B5/A   B♭   Em

111   134211   1333   1333   33   1333   23

Intro

| Esus4 G | D C B5/A | Esus4 G | D   C |

Verse 1

Esus4 G   D   C B5/A
Polly wants a cracker,

Esus4   G   D   C   B5/A
I think I should get off her ___ first.

Esus4   G   D   C B5/A
I think she wants some water

Esus4 G   D   C
To put out the blow ___ torch.

Chorus 1

D C   G B♭
It isn't me.   Have a seed.

D C   G B♭
Let me clip   dirty wings.

D C   G B♭
Let me take a ride.   Cut yourself.

D C   G B♭
Want some help,   please myself.

D C   G B♭
Got some rope,   have been told.

D C   G B♭
Promise you   have been true.

D C   G B♭
Let me take a ride.   Cut yourself.

D C   G B♭
Want some help,   please myself.

| *Interlude 1* | `|Esus4 G |D  C B5/A |Esus4 G |D    C    |` |

Verse 2

Esus4 G   D   C B5/A
Polly wants a cracker,

Esus4 G   D   C   B5/A
Maybe she would like some ___ food.

Esus4   G   D   C B5/A
She'll ask me to un - tie her.

Esus4 G   D   C
Chase would be nice for a few.

Chorus 2   *Repeat Chorus 1*

| *Interlude 2* | `|Esus4 N.C.(G) |(D)  (C) |(Em)   (G) |(D)  (C)  |` |

                            Polly said.

Verse 3

Esus4 G   D   C B5/A
Polly says her back hurts,

Esus4 G   D   C   B5/A
She's just as bored as ___ me.

Esus4 G   D   C   B5/A
She caught me off my ___ guard.

Esus4 G   D   C
A - mazes me, the will of instinct.

Chorus 3

D C   G B♭
It isn't me.   Have a seed.

D C   G B♭
Let me clip   dirty wings.

D C   G   B♭
Let me take a ride.   Cut yourself.

D C   G B♭
Want some help,   please myself.

D C   G B♭
Got some rope,   have been told.

D C   G B♭
Promise you   have been true.

D C   G   B♭
Let me take a ride.   Cut yourself.

D C   G B♭   Esus4
Want some help,   please myself.

Rape Me

Words and Music by
Kurt Cobain

Melody:

Rape   me. _____

Tune down 1/2 step:
(low to high) E♭ - A♭ - D♭ - G♭ - B♭ - E♭

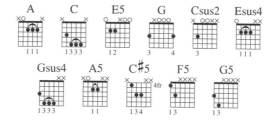

Intro	‖: A C │ E5 G :‖
	A Csus2 Esus4 Gsus4
Verse 1	Rape me.
	A C Esus4 G
	Rape me, ___ my friend.
	A C Esus4 G
	Rape me.
	A C E5 G
	Rape me ___ again.
	A C E5 G
Chorus 1	I'm not the on - ly one. I,
	A C E5 G
	I'm not the on - ly one. I,
	A C E5 G
	I'm not the on - ly one. I,
	A C E5 G
	I'm not the on - ly one.

Verse 2

A5   C E5 G
Hate me.

A5   C E5 G
Do it and do it again.

A5   C E5 G
Waste me.

A5   C   E5 G
Rape me, my friend.

Chorus 2   *Repeat Chorus 1*

Bridge

C#5   A5 N.C.
  My fav'rite inside source.

C#5   A5 N.C.
  I'll kiss your open sores.

C#5   A5 N.C.
  Appreciate your concern.

C#5   A5 N.C.
  You're gonna stink and burn.

| F5 | G5 | E5 | | |

Verse 3

A   C E5 G
Rape me.

A   C   E5 G
Rape me, my friend.

A   C E5 G
Rape me.

A   C E5 G
Rape me again.

Chorus 3   *Repeat Chorus 1*

Outro

  A   C
||: Rape me. (Rape me.)

E5   G
Rape me. (Rape me.) :|| *Play 4 times*

A5
Rape me.

Scentless Apprentice

Words and Music by Kurt Cobain,
Krist Novoselic and David Grohl

Melody:

Like most ba - bies smell _ like but - ter,

Drop D tuning, down 1/2 step:
(low to high) D♭ - A♭ - D♭ - G♭ - B♭ - E♭

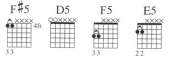

F#5   D5   F5   E5

Intro

|N.C. | |

||:(F#5) (D5)(F#5) (D5)(F#5) (D5)(F#5) (D5) :|| *Play 3 times*

| (F#5) (D5)(F#5) (D5)(F#5) (D5)(F#5) |

||: F#5 D5 F#5 D5 F#5 D5 F#5 D5 :|| *Play 4 times*

Verse 1

N.C.(F#5)
Like most babies

                F#5 D5 F#5 D5 F#5   D5 F#5 D5
Smell like butter,

N.C.(F#5)
His smell smelled

                F#5 D5 F#5 D5 F#5   D5 F#5 D5
Like no other.

N.C.(F#5)
He was born

                       F#5 D5 F#5 D5 F#5   D5 F#5 D5
A scentless and senseless.

N.C.(F#5)
He was born

                F#5 D5 F#5 D5 F#5   D5 F#5
A scentless apprentice.

Pre-Chorus 1 |N.C.(F5) (E5)(D5) |(F5)   (E5)(D5) |(F5)   (E5)(D5) |(F5) |

Chorus 1 |N.C.(F#5) (D5)(F#5) (D5)(F#5) (D5)(F#5)(D5) |
    Go _____ a - way, _

|(F#5) (D5)(F#5) (D5)(F#5)   (D5)(F#5) (D5) |
    _____   Get a - way, _

|(F#5) (D5)(F#5) (D5)(F#5)   (D5)(F#5) (D5) |
    _____   Get a - way! _

|(F#5) (D5)(F#5) (D5)(F#5)   (D5)(F#5) |
    _____

||:F#5   D5 F#5   D5 F#5   D5 F#5 D5   :||

Verse 2
N.C.(F#5)
Ev'ry wet nurse

                F#5 D5 F#5 D5 F#5   D5 F#5 D5
Refused to feed him.

   N.C.(F#5)
E - lectrolytes

               F#5 D5 F#5 D5 F#5   D5 F#5 D5
Smell like semen.

   N.C.(F#5)
I promise not to sell

                F#5 D5 F#5 D5 F#5   D5 F#5 D5
Your perfumed secrets.

      N.C.(F#5)
There are countless formulas

              F#5 D5 F#5 D5   F#5 D5 F#5
For pressing flowers.

Pre-Chorus 2   *Repeat Pre-Chorus 1*

Chorus 2 |N.C.(F#5) (D5)(F#5) (D5)(F#5) (D5)(F#5) (D5) |
    Go _____ a - way, _

|(F#5) (D5)(F#5) (D5)(F#5)   (D5)(F#5) (D5) |
    _____   Go a - way, _

|(F#5) (D5)(F#5) (D5)(F#5)   (D5)(F#5) (D5) |
    _____   Go a - way! _

|(F#5) (D5)(F#5) (D5)(F#5)   (D5)(F#5) |
    _____

Guitar Solo   ‖:N.C.(F#5) (D5)(F#5) (D5)(F#5) (D5)(F#5) (D5) :‖ *Play 7 times*
| (F#5) (D5)(F#5) (D5)(F#5) (D5) D5 |

Interlude   ‖: F#5   D5   F#5   D5   F#5   D5   F#5   D5   :‖ *Play 4 times*

Verse 3
N.C.(F#5)
I lie in the soil

            F#5 D5 F#5 D5 F#5   D5 F#5 D5
And fertilize mushrooms.

N.C.(F#5)
Leak - in' out gas fumes

          F#5 D5 F#5 D5 F#5   D5 F#5 D5
Made into perfume.

N.C.(F#5)
You can't fire me,

         F#5 D5 F#5 D5 F#5   D5 F#5 D5
'Cause I quit.

N.C.(F#5)
Throw me in the fire,

         F#5 D5 F#5 D5 F#5   D5 F#5 D5
I won't throw a fit.

Pre-Chorus 3   *Repeat Pre-Chorus 1*

Chorus 3
|N.C.(F#5) (D5)(F#5) (D5)(F#5) (D5)(F#5) (D5) |
  Hey! _____ Go a - way! ___

‖:(F#5) (D5)(F#5) (D5)(F#5)   (D5)(F#5) (D5)
_____ Go a - way! _ :‖ *Play 6 times*

|F#5 |N.C.   ‖
_____

Serve the Servants

Words and Music by
Kurt Cobain

Melody:

Teen-age angst _ has paid off well. _

Tune down 1/2 step:
(low to high) E♭ - A♭ - D♭ - G♭ - B♭ - E♭

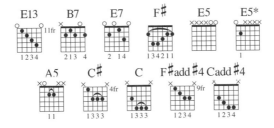

E13 B7 E7 F♯ E5 E5*

A5 C♯ C F♯add♯4 Cadd♯4

Intro

```
|E13      |         |
||:N.C.(B7) |(E7)    |F♯  E5  |E5*  E5 :||
```

Verse 1

N.C.(B7)   (E7)
Teenage angst has paid off well.

F♯   E5   E5* E5
Now I'm bored and old.

N.C.(B7)   (E7)
Self appointed judg - es judge

F♯   E5   E5* E5
More than they have sold.

N.C.(B7)   (E7)
If she floats then she ___ is not

 F♯   E5   E5* E5
A witch like we had thought.

N.C.(B7)   (E7)
A down payment on ___ another

F♯   E5   E5* E5
One at Salem's lot.

Chorus 1

A5   C#
Serve the serv - ants, oh no.

A5   C#
Serve the serv - ants, oh no.

A5   C#
Serve the serv - ants, oh no.

A5   C#
Serve the serv - ants.

      F#   C   F#add#4
That leg - endary divorce ___ is such a bore.

Verse 2

N.C.(B7)   (E7)
As my bones grew, they did hurt.

F#   E5   E5* E5
They hurt really bad.

N.C.(B7)   (E7)
I tried hard to have ___ a father,

      F#   E5   E5* E5
But in - stead I had a dad.

N.C.(B7)   (E7)
I just want you to ___ know that I

F#   E5   E5* E5
Don't hate you anymore.

N.C.(B7)   (E7)
There is nothing I ___ could say

      F# E5   E5* E5
That I have - n't thought before.

Chorus 2

A5   C#
    Serve the serv - ants, oh no.

A5   C#
    Serve the serv - ants, oh no.

A5   C#
    Serve the serv - ants, oh no.

             C#
Serve the serv - ants.

       F#   C   C#
That leg - endary divorce ___ is such a bore.

Guitar Solo

‖:N.C.(B7) │(E7)   │F# E5 │E5* E5 :‖ *Play 4 times*

Chorus 3

A5   C#
    Serve the serv - ants, oh no.

A5   C#
    Serve the serv - ants, oh no.

A5   C#
    Serve the serv - ants, oh no.

A5   C#
    Serve the serv - ants, oh no.

A5   C#
    Serve the serv - ants, oh no.

A5   C#
    Serve the serv - ants, oh no.

A5   C#
    Serve the serv - ants.

       F#   C   Cadd#4
That leg - endary divorce ___ is such a bore.

School

Words and Music by
Kurt Cobain

Melody:

Would-n't you be - lieve it, it's just ___ my ___ luck,

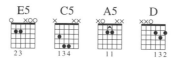

E5	C5	A5	D
2 3	1 3 4	1 1	1 3 2

Intro ‖: N.C.(E5) | :‖ *Play 4 times*

Verse 1

N.C.(E5)
Wouldn't you believe it, it's just my luck,

Wouldn't you believe it, it's just my luck,

Wouldn't you believe it, it's just my luck,

Wouldn't you believe it, it's just my luck.

Chorus 1

C5 A5   E5 D
    No recess.   No recess.

C5 A5   N.C.(E5)
    No recess.

Verse 2   *Repeat Verse 1*

Chorus 2   *Repeat Chorus 1*

Guitar Solo ‖: N.C.(E5) | :‖ *Play 4 times*

Verse 3

N.C.(E5)
You're in my school again, you're in my school again,

You're in our school again, you're in our school again,

You're in our school again, you're in our school again,

You're in our school again, you're in our school again.

Chorus 3

C5 A5   E5 D
   No recess.   No recess.

C5 A5   E5 D
   No recess.   No recess.

C5 A5   E5 D
   No recess.   No recess.

C5 A5
   No recess.

Sliver

Words and Music by
Kurt Cobain

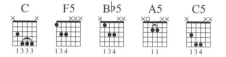

C   F5   B♭5   A5   C5

Intro

| N.C.(C) (F5) | (C) (B♭5) |
| (C)   (F5) | (C) (A5) |

Verse 1

N.C.(C)   (F5)   (C) (A5)
  Mom and Dad went to   a show.

(C)   (F5)   (C)   (A5)
  They dropped me off at Grand - pa Joe's.

(C)   (F5)   (C)   (A5)
  I kicked and screamed, said please, ___ no.

Chorus 1

A5   C5
||: Grandma take me home.

A5   C5
Grandma take me home.   :|| *Play 4 times*

Verse 2

C   F5   C   A5
  Had to eat my din - ner there.

C   F5   C   A5
  Mashed potatoes and stuff like that.

C   F5   C   A5
  I could - n't chew my meat   good.

Chorus 2

Repeat Chorus 1

Verse 3

C   F5   C   A5
Said, well good, just stop your cryin'.

C   F5   C   A5
Go outside and ride your bike.

C   F5   C   A5
That's what I did, I kicked my toe.

Chorus 3

Repeat Chorus 1

Verse 4

C
After dinner I had ice cream.

I fell asleep and watched TV.

I woke up in my mother's arms.

Outro-Chorus

    A5   C5
‖: Grandma take me home.

A5   C5
Grandma take me home. :‖ *Play 9 times*

A5   C5   A5   C5   C
Grandma take me home. Want to be alone.

Smells Like Teen Spirit

Words and Music by Kurt Cobain,
Krist Novoselic and Dave Grohl

Melody:

Load up __ on guns __ and bring __ your friends. __

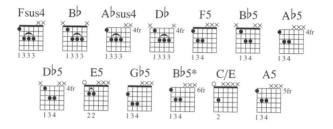

Fsus4 Bb Absus4 Db F5 Bb5 Ab5

Db5 E5 Gb5 Bb5* C/E A5

Intro	‖: **Fsus4** **Bb** |**Absus4** **Db** :‖ *Play 6 times*
	‖: **N.C.(F5)** **(Bb5)** |**(Ab5)** **(Db5)** :‖
Verse 1	**N.C.(F5)** **(Bb5)** **(Ab5)** **(Db5)** Load up ____ on guns ___ and bring ___ your friends.
	(F5) **(Bb5)** **(Ab5)** **(Db5)** It's fun ____ to lose ____ and to ____ pretend.
	(F5) **(Bb5)** **(Ab5)** **(Db5)** She's o - verbored ____ and self - assured.
	(F5) **(Bb5)** **(Ab5)** **(Db5)** Oh no, ____ I know ____ a dirt - y word.
Pre-Chorus 1	**(F5)** **(Bb5)** **(Ab5)** **(Db5)** ‖: Hello, ____ hello, ____ hello, ____ how low? :‖ *Play 3 times*
	(F5) **(Bb5)** **(Ab5)** **(Db5)** Hello, ____ hello, ____ hello.

Chorus 1

              Fsus4   **B♭**   **A♭sus4**   **D♭**
With the lights ___ out it's less dan - g'rous.

                  Fsus4   **B♭** **A♭sus4**   **D♭**
Here we are ___ now, entertain ___ us.

          Fsus4 B♭   **A♭sus4**   **D♭**
I feel stu - pid and conta - gious.

                  Fsus4   **B♭**   **A♭sus4**   **D♭**
Here we are ___ now, entertain ___ us.

          Fsus4 B♭ **A♭sus4 D♭**
A mulat - o, an albi - no,

           Fsus4 B♭ **A♭sus4 D♭**
A mosqui - to, my libi - do.   Yeah.

Bridge 1

| **F5** **E5** **F5** **G♭5** **N.C.** | **F5** **E5** **F5** **B♭5*** **A♭5** **C/E**
                  Yay,

| **F5** **E5** **F5** **G♭5** **N.C.** | **F5** **E5** **F5** **B♭5*** **A5** **A♭5**
                  Yay.

Interlude 1

‖: **N.C.(F5)** **(B♭5)** | **(A♭5)**   **(D♭5)**   :‖

Verse 2

N.C.(F5)   **(B♭5)**   **(A♭5)** **(D♭5)**
  I'm worse ___ at what ___ I ___ do best,

(F5)   **(B♭5)**   **(A♭5)**   **(D♭5)**
  And for ___ this gift ___ I feel ___ blessed.

(F5)   **(B♭5)**   **(A♭5)**   **(D♭5)**
  Our lit - tle group ___ has al - ways been

(F5)   **(B♭5)**   **(A♭5)**   **(D♭5)**
  And al - ways will ___ until ___ the end.

Pre-Chorus 2   *Repeat Pre-Chorus 1*

Chorus 2   *Repeat Chorus 1*

Bridge 2   *Repeat Bridge 1*

Guitar Solo   ‖: **Fsus4** **B♭** | **A♭sus4** **D♭**   :‖ *Play 8 times*

Interlude 2   *Repeat Interlude 1*

Verse 3
    N.C.(F5)(B♭5)   (A♭5)   (D♭5)
        And I ___ forget ___ just why ___ I taste.

    (F5)   (B♭5)   (A♭5)   (D♭5)
        Oo yeah, ___ I guess ___ it makes ___ you smile.

    (F5)   (B♭5)   (A♭5)   (D♭5)
        I found ___ it hard, ___ it's hard ___ to find.

    (F5)   (B♭5)   (A♭5) (D♭5)
        Oh well, ___ whatev - er, nev - er mind.

Pre-Chorus 3   *Repeat Pre-Chorus 1*

                  Fsus4   B♭   A♭sus4   D♭
Chorus 3   With the lights ___ out it's less dan - g'rous.

               Fsus4   B♭   A♭sus4   D♭
    Here we are ___ now, enter - tain ___ us.

            Fsus4 B♭   A♭sus4   D♭
    I feel stu - pid and conta - gious.

               Fsus4   B♭   A♭sus4   D♭
    Here we are ___ now, entertain ___ us.

            Fsus4 B♭ A♭sus4   D♭
    A mulat - o, an albi - no,

            Fsus4 B♭   A♭sus4
    A mosqui - to, my libi - do.

Outro
            Fsus4 B♭   A♭sus4   D♭
    A de - nial,   a de - nial,

            Fsus4 B♭   A♭sus4   D♭
    A de - nial,   a de - nial,

            Fsus4 B♭   A♭sus4   D♭
    A de - nial,   a de - nial,

            Fsus4 B♭   A♭sus4   D♭
    A de - nial,   a de - nial,

            F5
    A de - nial!

Something in the Way

Words and Music by
Kurt Cobain

Melody:

Un-der - neath _the bridge, _ tarp has sprung _a leak. _

Drop D tuning, down 1/2 step:
(low to high) D♭ - A♭ - D♭ - G♭ - B♭ - E♭

F#5   D5   D5*

Intro
‖: F#5 D5 |F#5 D5 :‖

Verse 1

F#5   D5   F#5   D5
Underneath the bridge, ____ tarp has sprung a leak.

        F#5   D5   F#5   D5
And the animals I've trapped ____ have all become my pets.

        F#5   D5   F#5   D5
And I'm living off of grass ____ and the drippings from the ceil - ing.

F#5   D5   F#5   D5
It's okay to eat fish ____ 'cause they don't have any feel - ings.

Chorus 1

        F#5   D5* F#5 D5*
‖: Something in the way. ____ Mm.

F#5   D5*   F#5 D5*
Something in the way, ____ yeah. Mm.   :‖ *Play 3 times*

Verse 2   *Repeat Verse 1*

Chorus 2

        F#5   D5* F#5 D5*
‖: Something in the way. ____ Mm.

F#5   D5*   F#5 D5*
Something in the way, ____ yeah. Mm.   :‖ *Play 4 times*

Spank Through

Words and Music by
Kurt Cobain

Melody:

Mumbled: This song is   for lov-ers out there

Chord diagrams: A   G   D5   A5   G5   D5/A
F5   G6   G5*   E5   B5   Bb5

Intro

|A   G   D5 |A   G |A   G   D5 |A   G |
|A   G   D5 |A5   G5 |A5   G5 D5 |A   G5 |

Verse 1

A5   G5   D5   A5 G5
This song is for lov - ers out there

A5   G5   D5   A5 G5
And the little light ____ in the trees.

A5   G5   D5   A5 G5
And all the flowers have gin - givi - tis

A5   G5   D5   A5 G5
And the birds fly happily.

A5   G5   D5   A5   G5
We're to - gether once again, my love.

A5   G5   D5   A5 G5
I need you back, oh baby, ba - by.

Chorus 1

D5/A   A5
I can't explain ____ just why

   F5   G6
We lost it from the start.

D5/A   A5
Living without ____ you, girl,

   F5   G5*
You only break my heart. Yeah!

Interlude 1

||: N.C.(E5) (G5) |(E5)   (G5)   :||

Verse 2

        N.C.(E5) (G5)   (E5)   (G5)
I can feel it.   I can hold it.

     (E5) (G5)   (E5)   (G5)
I can bend it,   shape it and mold it.

       (E5) (G5)   (E5)   (G5)
I can cut it.   I can taste it,

(E5)   (G5)   (E5)   (G5)
Spank it,   beat it till you,   ah, wait here now.

Chorus 2

B5   B♭5 A5 D5   A5 B♭5
 I been look - ing for   days now,

B5   B♭5 A5 D5   N.C. A5 B♭5
 Always hear - ing the same ol'.

B5   B♭5 A5 D5   A5 B♭5
 City boy, won't you spank thru?

B5   G5*   F5
 I can make it do things you wouldn't think you ever could.

Interlude 2   *Repeat Interlude 1*

Verse 3

        N.C.(E5) (G5)   (E5)   (G5)
I can feel it.   I can hold it.

(E5) (G5)   (E5)   (G5)
Bend it,   shape it and mold it.

     (E5) (G5)   (E5)   (G5)
He can cut it.   He can taste it,

(E5)   (G5)   (E5)   (G5)
Spank it,   beat it till you,   ah, wait here now.

Chorus 3   *Repeat Chorus 2*

Interlude 3   *Repeat Interlude 1*

Guitar Solo   ‖: **N.C.(E5) (G5)** | **(E5)   (G5)** :‖ *Play 6 times*

Chorus 4

B5   B♭5 A5 D5   A5 B♭5
 I been look - ing for   days now,

B5   B♭5 A5 D5   N.C. A5 B♭5
 Always hear - ing the same ol'.

B5   B♭5 A5 D5   A5 B♭5
 City boy, won't you spank thru?

B5   G5*   F5
 I can make it do things you wouldn't think you ever could.

G5*   F5   E5
 You won't think you ever could.

Stain

Words and Music by
Kurt Cobain

Melody:

Well, he nev-er bleeds _ and he

Drop D tuning:
(low to high) D-A-D-G-B-E

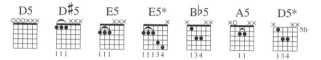

D5   D#5   E5   E5*   Bb5   A5   D5*

Intro

| D5   D#5 |
| E5 E5* D5 D#5 | E5 E5* D5 D#5 |
‖: E5 E5* D5 D#5 | E5 E5* D5 D#5 :‖ *Play 3 times*

Verse 1

      D#5 E5 E5*
Well, he ne - ver bleeds

D5 D#5   E5 E5*
And he nev - er fucks,

D5 D#5   E5 E5*
And he nev - er leaves

D5   D#5   E5 E5*
'Cause he's got bad luck.

D5 D#5   E5 E5*
Well, he nev - er   reads

D5 D#5   E5 E5*
And he nev - er roughs,

D5 D#5   E5 E5*
And he nev - er   sleeps

D5   D#5   E5   E5*   D5 D#5
'Cause he's got   bad   luck. Yeah.

Chorus 1

Bb5 A5   D5*
        I'm a stain.

Bb5 A5   D5
        I'm a stain.

Bb5 A5   D5*
        I'm a stain.

Bb5 A5   D5   D#5
        I'm a stain.

Interlude 1

‖: D#5 E5 E5* D5 D#5 | E5 E5* D5 D#5 :‖

Verse 2

Repeat Verse 1

Chorus 2

Bb5 A5   D5*
        I'm a stain.

Bb5 A5   D5
        I'm a stain.

Bb5 A5   D5*
        I'm a stain.

Bb5 A5   D5   D#5
        I'm a stain. Uh.

Guitar Solo

‖: D#5 E5 E5* D5 D#5 | E5 E5* D5 D#5 :‖ *Play 8 times*

Chorus 3

Repeat Chorus 2

Interlude 2

Repeat Interlude 1

Verse 3

Repeat Verse 1

Chorus 4

  Bb5 A5   D5*
‖:   I'm a stain.

Bb5 A5   D5
       I'm a stain. :‖ *Play 3 times*

Bb5 A5   D5*
       I'm a stain.

Bb5 A5   D5
       I'm a stain.

Stay Away

Words and Music by
Kurt Cobain

Melody:

Mon-key see, mon-key do. I don't know why! __

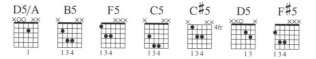

D5/A   B5   F5   C5   C#5   D5   F#5

Intro

‖: N.C.(D5/A) (B5) (F5) | (C5) |
| (D5/A)   (B5) (F5) | (C5) (C#5) :‖
| D5/A B5 F5 | C5 | D5/A B5 F5 | C5 C#5 |
| D5/A B5 F5 | C5 C#5 | D5/A B5 F5 | C5 |

Verse 1

N.C.(D5/A) (B5)   (F5)   (C5)
Monkey see, ___ monkey do. ___ I don't know why!

  (D5/A)   (B5)   (F5)   (C5)
I'd rather be ___ dead then cool. ___ I don't know why!

(D5/A)   (B5)   (F5)   (C5)
Ev'ry line ___ ends in rhyme. ___ I don't know why!

(D5/A)   (B5)   (F5)   (C5)
Less is more, ___ love is blind. ___ I don't know why!

Chorus 1

D5/A B5 F5 C5   C#5
Stay, _____   stay a - way!

D5/A B5 F5 C5   C#5
              Stay a - way!

D5/A B5 F5 C5   C#5
              Stay a - way!

D5/A B5 F5 C5

Verse 2

N.C.(D5/A)   (B5)   (F5)   (C5)
Give an inch, ___ take a smile. ___ I don't know why!

(D5/A)   (B5)   (F5)   (C5)
Fashion shits, ___ fashion style. ___ I don't know why!

(D5/A)   (B5)   (F5)   (C5)
Throw it out ___ and keep it in. ___ I don't know why!

(D5/A)   (B5)   (F5)   (C5)
Have to have ___ poison skin. ___ I don't know why!

Chorus 2   *Repeat Chorus 1*

Bridge 1   ‖: D5 | | F$\sharp$5 | :‖
                                              I don't know why!

Chorus 3   *Repeat Chorus 1*

Verse 3   *Repeat Verse 1*

Chorus 4   *Repeat Chorus 1*

Bridge 2   *Repeat Bridge 1*

Chorus 5   *Repeat Chorus 1*

Interlude   ‖: N.C.(D5/A) (B5) (F5) | (C5) (C$\sharp$5) :‖ *Play 3 times*
                  | (D5/A) (B5) (F5) | (C5) (C$\sharp$5) |
                                                   Ah!

                  D5/A B5 F5 C5   C$\sharp$5
Outro-Chorus ‖:   Stay a - way! :‖ *Play 5 times*
                  D5/A B5 F5 C5   C$\sharp$5   D5/A
                              God is gay!

Territorial Pissings

Words and Music by
Kurt Cobain and Chet Powers

Melody:

When I was an al - i - en, _____

Am$^6_9$ Asus4   F   D   A   A5

Intro

N.C.
Come on, people now, smile on your brother.

Am$^6_9$
Ev'rybody get together, try to love one another right now.

| Asus4 | F | D | | |
| Asus4 | F | D | | |

Mm.

Verse 1

A   F   D
When I was an alien,

A   F   D
Cultures weren't o - pinions.

Chorus 1

A   F   D
Gotta find a way to find a way when I'm there.

A   F   D
Gotta find a way, a better way, I had better wait.

Verse 2

A F D
Never met a wise man;

A F D
If so it's a woman.

GUITAR CHORD SONGBOOK

Chorus 2

    A   F   D
‖: Gotta find a way to find a way when I'm there.

A   F   D
Gotta find a way, a better way, I had better wait. :‖

Interlude

| A | | | |
| | | | D |

Verse 3

N.C.(A) (F)   (D)
Just be - cause you're paranoid,

(A)   (F)   (D)   N.C.
Don't mean they're not after you.

Chorus 3

    A   F   D
‖: Gotta find a way to find a way when I'm there.

A   F   D
Gotta find a way, a better way, I had better wait. :‖ *Play 3 times*

A   F   D
Gotta find a way, a better way, when I'm there.

A   F   D   A5
Gotta find a way, a better way, I had better wait. Yeah.

Very Ape

Words and Music by
Kurt Cobain

Melody:

I am bur-ied up   to   my   neck   in

Tune down 1/2 step:
(low to high) Eb - Ab - Db - Gb - Bb - Eb

G5   A5   Bb5   Bb   G   A   F5

C5   B5   C5*   Eb5   G5*   F#5

Intro

G5 |A5 G5 Bb5 G5 |A5 G5 Bb5 G5 |A5 G5 Bb G |

|A G Bb5 G |A G5 Bb5 G5 |A5 G5 Bb5 G5 |

|A5 G5 Bb5 G5 |A5 G5 Bb G |

Verse 1

A G5 Bb5   G A   G Bb
I am buried up ___ to my ___ neck

    G   A   G5 Bb5   G5 A5 G5 Bb5 G
In ___   con - tra - diction - airy ___ flies.

A G5 Bb5   G5 A5   G5 Bb5   G5
I take pride as the king of il - literature.

    F5   C5 B5 G5
I'm very ape ___ and very nice.

Interlude 1

|A5 G5 Bb5 G5 |A5 G5 Bb5 G |

|A G5 Bb G5 |A G5 Bb G |

Verse 2

A G5 Bb5   G A   G5
If you ever need ___ anything,

Bb5   G5 A5   G5 Bb5   G5
Please don't ___   hes - i - tate to ask

A5   G5 Bb5 G
Someone else ___ first.

A   G5 Bb5   G A   G5 Bb5 G5
I'm too busy act - ing like I'm not ___ naïve.

    F5   C5 B5 G5
I've seen it all. ___ I was here first.

Interlude 2	|A5 G5 Bb5 G5 |A5 G5 Bb5 G5 | |A5 G5 Bb5 G5 |A5 G5 Bb5 G5|

Interlude 2

|A5 G5 Bb5 G5 |A5 G5 Bb5 G5 |

|A5 G5 Bb5 G5 |A5 G5 Bb5 G5|

Chorus 1

|A5 C5* Eb5 |

G5* G5 F#5 G5 A5   C5* Eb5
Out of   the ground,

G5* G5 F#5 G5 A5 C5* Eb5
In - to   the sky.

G5* G5 F#5 G5 A5 C5* Eb5
Out of   the sky,

G5* G5 F#5 G5
In - to   the dirt.

Interlude 3

|A5 G5 Bb5 G5 |A   G5 Bb   G |

|A   G5 Bb5 G5 |A5 G5 Bb   G |

Verse 3 *Repeat Verse 2*

Interlude 4 *Repeat Interlude 2*

Chorus 2

|A5 C5* Eb5 |

G5* G5 F#5 G5 A5   C5* Eb5
Out of   the ground,

G5* G5 F#5 G5 A5 C5* Eb5
In - to   the sky.

G5* G5 F#5 G5 A5 C5* Eb5
Out of   the sky,

G5* G5 F#5 G5 A5 C5* Eb5
In - to   the dirt.

G5* G5 F#5 G5 A5   C5* Eb5
Out of   the ground,

G5* G5 F#5 G5 A5 C5 Eb5
In - to   the sky.

G5* G5 F#5 G5 A5 C5* Eb5
Out of   the sky,

G5* G5 F#5 G5 A5
In - to   the dirt.

You Know You're Right

Words and Music by
Kurt Cobain

Tune down 1/2 step:
(low to high) E♭ - A♭ - D♭ - G♭ - B♭ - E♭

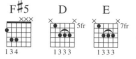

Melody:

I will nev - er both - er you

F#5   D   E

Intro

‖: N.C.(F#5) | :‖

‖: F#5 | :‖

Verse 1

F#5
I will never bother you.

I will never promise to.

I will never follow you.

I will never bother you.

D
Never speak a word again.

E
I will crawl away for good.

Verse 2

F#5
I will move away from here.

You won't be afraid of fear.

And I thought I was fooled into this,

And always knew it would come to this.

D
Things have never been so swell.

E
I have never felt or failed.

Chorus 1	**F#5** Hey!　　Hey!
	D　　E　　　　　　　　**F#5** Hey! ＿ You know you're ＿＿right.
	You know you're right. You know you're right.
Verse 3	**N.C.(F#5)** So, woman, come inside.
	I no longer have to hide.
	Let's talk about someone else.
	Steaming Sue begins to melt.
	D Nothing really bothers her,
	E She just wants to love herself.
Verse 4	*Repeat Verse 2*
Chorus 2	**F#5** Hey!　　Hey!
	Hey!　　Hey!
	D　　E　　　　　　　　**F#5** Hey! ＿ You know you're ＿＿ right.
	‖: You know you're right. You know you're right. :‖ *Play 8 times*
	N.C. Hey!
Outro	|N.C.(F#5)　|　　　|　　|　　　| |　　　|　　|　　‖

Guitar Chord Songbooks

Each book includes complete lyrics, chord symbols, and guitar chord diagrams.

00701787 **Acoustic Hits** $14.99	00699732 **Elton John** . . . . $15.
00699540 **Acoustic Rock** $21.99	00130337 **Ray LaMontagne** . . . . $12.
00699914 **Alabama** $14.95	00700973 **Latin Songs** . . . . $14.
00699566 **The Beach Boys** $19.99	00701043 **Love Songs** . . . . $14.
00699562 **The Beatles** $17.99	00701704 **Bob Marley** . . . . $17.
00702585 **Bluegrass** $14.99	00125332 **Bruno Mars** . . . . $12.
00699648 **Johnny Cash** $17.99	00385035 **Paul McCartney** . . . . $16.
00699539 **Children's Songs** $16.99	00701146 **Steve Miller** . . . . $12.
00699536 **Christmas Carols** $12.99	00701801 **Modern Worship** . . . . $16.
00119911 **Christmas Songs** $14.99	00699734 **Motown** . . . . $17.
00699567 **Eric Clapton** $19.99	00148273 **Willie Nelson** . . . . $17.
00699598 **Classic Rock** $18.99	00699762 **Nirvana** . . . . $16.
00703318 **Coffeehouse Hits** $14.99	00699752 **Roy Orbison** . . . . $17.
00699534 **Country** $17.99	00103013 **Peter, Paul & Mary** . . . . $19.
00700609 **Country Favorites** $14.99	00699883 **Tom Petty** . . . . $15.
00140859 **Country Hits** $14.99	00139116 **Pink Floyd** . . . . $14.
00700608 **Country Standards** $12.95	00699538 **Pop/Rock** . . . . $16.
00699636 **Cowboy Songs** $19.99	00699634 **Praise & Worship** . . . . $14.
00701786 **Creedence Clearwater Revival** $16.99	00699633 **Elvis Presley** . . . . $17.
00148087 **Jim Croce** $14.99	00702395 **Queen** . . . . $14.
00701609 **Crosby, Stills & Nash** $16.99	00699710 **Red Hot Chili Peppers** . . . . $19.
02501697 **John Denver** $17.99	00137716 **The Rolling Stones** . . . . $17.
00700606 **Neil Diamond** $19.99	00701147 **Bob Seger** . . . . $12.
00295786 **Disney** $17.99	00121011 **Carly Simon** . . . . $14.
00699888 **The Doors** $17.99	00699921 **Sting** . . . . $17.
00122917 **Eagles** $17.99	00263755 **Taylor Swift** . . . . $16.
00699916 **Early Rock** $14.99	00123860 **Three Chord Acoustic Songs** . . $14.
00699541 **Folksongs** $14.99	00699720 **Three Chord Songs** . . . . $17.
00699651 **Folk Pop Rock** $17.99	00119236 **Two-Chord Songs** . . . . $16.
00115972 **40 Easy Strumming Songs** $16.99	00137744 **U2** . . . . $14.
00701611 **Four Chord Songs** $14.99	00700607 **Hank Williams** . . . . $16.
00702501 **Glee** $14.99	00120862 **Stevie Wonder** . . . . $14.
00700463 **Gospel Hymns** $14.99	
00699885 **Grand Ole Opry®** $16.95	
00139461 **Grateful Dead** $14.99	
00103074 **Green Day** $14.99	
00701044 **Irish Songs** $14.99	
00137847 **Michael Jackson** $14.99	
00699632 **Billy Joel** $19.99	

Visit Hal Leonard online at **www.halleonard.com**

*Prices, contents, and availability
subject to change without notice.*

1
6/9;